When I Was Seventeen

Marianne LaValle-Vincent

Cyberwit.net
HIG 45 Kaushambi Kunj, Kalindipuram
Allahabad - 211011 (U.P.) India
http://www.cyberwit.net
Tel: +(91) 9415091004 +(91) (532) 2552257
E-mail: info@cyberwit.net

Printed at Repro India Limited.

DEDICATION:

This collection of poems is built on memories. Some good—some not so good. Seventeen is an incredible age. For me, it was almost iconic. I dated the quarterback of the football team, was a cheerleader, was one of the "popular girls" and didn't have acne! A literal social butterfly, I had a hell of a lot of fun—yet there were hard times as well. Times that a 17-year-old girl thinks may be the end of life as we know it. Times that were replete with tears, break-ups, period cramps, bad haircuts, petty arguments, parental dissension and way too much homework.

High school is dreadful. It's amazing and incredible and full of love and fantasy and then it's dreadful again. It's the epitome of happiness and the dredges of hell. It's a rollercoaster ride that sometimes fills you with a feeling of euphoria and other times makes you want to throw in the towel. It's being the prom queen one day and the most hated girl in the world the next. You're in love—you're out of love. You're back in love—you wish he were dead. It all evens out. When you're a Senior—you've got a few advantages. You can kick a little underclassmen ass and get away with it and you can—at last—see a light at the end of the tunnel. Graduation and an end to this hell leads to the beginning of adulthood.

Seventeen is an age of simplicity. An age of wonderment and fulfillment. An age that promises the perfect future and the beautiful realization that your entire life is ahead of you. The age that offers both maturity and naivety—the age of "coming of age". For us back in 1967, 17 was the age that lasted an eternity because it was the age just before becoming legal! I'd like to be 17 for just a short time again. Boy—would I be better at it this time. But as they say—you just can't go home again!!

This book is dedicated to the class of 1967 and really, to all those Solvay grads that can relate to these experiences. To my friends and enemies. To my sorority sisters of Alpha Omega and those sisters in Lambda Phi and Zeta Epsilon. To all the girls and boys who thought themselves invisible. To those of us that decided life was just too hard, especially Joe Fournier. (his death left a hole in my heart that can never be repaired) To those I grew up with and those I grew apart from. I offer you this book in remembrance of what used to be. May each and every one of you find a little bit of nostalgia and love in these pages. Maybe for a while, we can go home again! I thank you for the most wonderful memories a woman could possibly have. We had it all!!! *When I was Seventeen!!!*

When I was 17, it was a very good year

It was a very good year for Solvay girls

And soft summer nights

We'd hide from the lights

On the Hazard green

When I was seventeen------

Contents

SMALL TOWN GIRL 7

THE HOUSE AT THE TOP OF THE HILL 9

THE INCOMPARABLE TWIN TREES 11

TANZELLA'S 13

SOLVAY FIELD DAYS 15

CLASSMATES 17

HELL NIGHT 19

WOODS ROAD 21

SANDY POND (AND MEMORIES OF JOE FOURNIER) 23

DONNA PIENKOWSKI'S GRANDMOTHER 25

RAH RAH SISS BOOM BAH 27

PEP RALLY 29

YOU CAN'T GO BACK AGAIN 31

I GOT THE MUSIC IN ME 33

SMOKER'S ROAD 35

THE EXTRORDINARY, ILLUSTRIOUS ONONDAGA LAKE 37

SMILE AND SAY CHEESE 39

BEARCAT ECHOES 41

LET US ENTERTAIN YOU 43

CHE CAFETERIA 45

THE EVER-DREADED DETENTION 47

THE NY STATE FAIR 49

FLIRTING AS AN ART FORM 51

THE MIRROR HAS TWO FACES 53

SURVIVAL OF THE FITTEST 55

ST. CECILIAS 57

A WANNA BE 59

THE MUCH-LOATHED GYM SUIT 61

SOLVAY POOL 63

TAKE FIVE 65

MY SUMMER AS A PARKS AND RECREATION SPECIALIST 67

POMP AND CIRCUMSTANCE 69

GUESS WHO'S COMING TO DINNER? 71

THE INNOCENCE OF SEVENTEEN (FOR JF) 73

SHE'S A DANCING MACHINE 75

THE BEST DRESSED STUDENTS 77

SHELTER FROM THE STORM 79

SEMI-FORMALS, PROMS AND OTHER SHINDIGS 81

UGLY DUCKLINGS 83

OBSESSIONS @ SEVENTEEN 85

WISHING ON A STAR 87

NOT A CARE IN THE WORLD 89

CONFESSIONS OF A VERY SHORT GIRL 91

THOSE PHENOMENAL THETA OMEGA GUYS 93

MEMORIES OF DARROW AVE 95

GOOD BYE TO INNOCENCE 97

EPILOGUE 99

SMALL TOWN GIRL

loafers and a pleated plaid skirt
white blouse with a peter-pan collar
hair teased in a flip and pink cotton candy lipstick
she strolls the halls hugging her books
notebook screaming the name of her true love
for all to see in bold letters drawn with black marker
homeroom antics set the mood for a typical Friday
as she daydreams about the weekend
mentally picking out her outfit and anticipating the inevitable
good nite whatever
the day drags on and she looks at the clock a million times
finally——lunch with him
a stale sandwich and some overly flirtatious talk
then a quick cigarette on smoker's road
3 pm— the last class of the day
he drives her home and they plan the evening
she lies to her parents since he's not what they'd want for her
but she doesn't care— she's in love
Genesee theater shows *The Graduate*
and she silently wishes she were more like Mrs. Robinson
pizza at twin trees—double cheese of course
and on to the parkway at Onondaga Lake
a steamy make-out session and home for the evening

the pregnancy lasted longer than the relationship
and she raised her son alone
marrying twice she never again found that passion
and she still cries herself to sleep some nights
as for him—

he remembers her and her white blouse with the peter pan collar
but mostly he remembers how she loved him
and he wonders what his son is like——who he looks like
and why he couldn't face his responsibilities

she sees him every time she looks at her son
and she marvels at her offspring's sensitivity and devotion to her
but she prays as he leaves to meet his girlfriend
that the apple falls a little bit farther from
his family tree

You've gotta win a little, lose a little—even have the blues a little
That's the glory of—that's the story of love

THE HOUSE AT THE TOP OF THE HILL

the house was fabulous
surrounded by trees and shrubbery
the in-ground pool was somewhat hidden
and the *Florida Room* was a sort of sanctuary for us girls
for it was there we gathered every Friday night
smoking parliament cigarettes and waiting for the guys to show up
sometimes we swam
or listened to music
and we discussed the important things in life
like shopping and the latest clothing trends
sometimes we all slept there—even the boys
encompassed by our innocence
yet counting the days until we could safely cross that unspoken line
and the few that did
would tell of the passion and sensuality
enticing those of us who clung to our virginity in typical Catholic fashion
forcing us to speculate in rated X dreams
what it would be like to finally say yes
and I yet I refused
more from fear of the unknown than purity
perhaps letting him get a base hit every once in a while
and we pierced our ears and tried new lipstick
teased our hair and read *Vogue*
fantasized about our future with the boy of the week
and maybe imbibed in an underaged drink or two
for nothing was forbidden in that glorious residence
it was all simply perfection
and then we went our separate ways
colleges and nursing schools

50 miles north and 70 miles south
but we'd meet there still—-every holiday and break
each of us sharing our new experiences
and picking up right where we left off
and when I think of my senior year
I find myself in that beautiful Florida room
and the memories soothe me and fill me with nostalgia
and—oh—how I wish I could go back
to that paradisiacal house on the hill

*****Those were the days my friend, we thought they'd
never end........*

THE INCOMPARABLE TWIN TREES

one of my favorite high school haunts
it was everyone's date night go-to
though we saw the same faces weekend after weekend
its magical ambiance kept us going back
dimly lit, it kept secrets better than a priest
while the seasoned bartenders looked the other way
should one of us have a quick cocktail
I loved to sit facing the door silently observing
each and every person that entered
though the pizza was practically world renowned
it was not the only reason we frequented this reputable night spot
the booths though worn and somewhat weathered
offered just the right amount of space for 6
we would squeeze in together
each of us thrilled with the closeness of our bodies
for we shared so much more than food in that beloved place
and the hours flew by as we talked about nothing
and those of us that were in love savored the moments spent there
as if it were a church
for we all became believers of this infamous watering hole
and like a magnet it pulled us in
again and again and again
and so many years later
when we were older but not too much wiser
we would return
seeking that illusion of yesteryear
still waiting for that special person to walk through the door

it still offers the best pizza around

and sometimes we still meet there
perhaps for a reunion or a cocktail at the bar
the walls may leak a secret or two
yet the magic remains though we silence those flashbacks
and we openly rejoice at the familiarity
for we remember as if it were last evening
the taste of youth and indulgence
that we shared in that restaurant we once called
our home away from home

If your lover didn't show—you'd find comfort in a pepperoni pizza

TANZELLA'S

for those of you who feel it's impossible to fall in love with a sandwich
you've obviously never known the delectable tastes of "Tanzy's"
this celebrated Italian treasure sat nestled in the middle of third street
unpretentious as it seemed it became a piece of history
the shelves were full of pastas and canned goods
and the glass coolers offered an array of specialty meats and cheeses
there were tomatoes and lettuce
garlic and cucumbers
to us it wasn't peasant food—it was the sustenance of our youth
which of us didn't salivate at the thought of capicola on the heel
of Italian bread
or a plain ole bologna sammy on white bread with mustard
and for 25 cents we filled our stomachs
and we listened to Tressa adding her earnings aloud as she
scribbled them on
brown deli paper faster than any modern computer
and she would lick the tip of the pencil
maybe just for effect
there were fudgesicles and creamsicles
red and black licorice
Pepsi in glass bottles
and we shared
everything
after filling our stomachs we'd smoke a few cigarettes
and if you were lucky enough to have a few extra coins
you'd take some goodies back to class for snacking

on Saturday's I would walk there at my mother's request
buying fresh Italian bread
and cold cuts for lunch

and I still remember the smell of that haven
for it was reminiscent of my heritage
we knew no bias back then
no bigotry or prejudice
we shared a love for the deliciousness of that little store
its offerings and its heavenly surroundings
for time spent there was happy and safe
and etched into our minds
like an exquisite tattoo
and will forever remain a mouthwatering five-star memory

*The class of '67 had foodgasms before we even knew what
they were*

SOLVAY FIELD DAYS

it was as if *Barnum and Bailey* visited our small town
and gave us three days of perfection without an entrance fee
we flocked there in groups
excited as much for the food
as we were for the games and rides
boyfriends displayed hidden talents
as they attempted to win prizes for the girls
and girls pretended to be virginal and pure
as they anticipated the long-awaited time alone
with one of the fraternity boys
the smell of fried foods permeated the air
and not a soul was concerned about the calories
or the ill-effects of cholesterol
we feasted on burgers and hot dogs
fried dough and French fries
while Mothers and Fathers who worked at the *"Tiger's Stand"*
supplied us with endless meatball subs and sodas
we would sneak behind one of the tents for a smoke and a beer
and walk the circumference of the field for hours
we held hands and laughed and kissed when we could
and rode the Ferris wheel in hopes of stopping at the top
it was a feeling of euphoria—being up there
probably the closest to heaven I'll ever be
for three days we met there
as if it were our job
parents, Aunts and Uncles
reveled in the activity
and it was as if this traditional festival
filled us with a sense of extraordinary being

for it was meant just for us
just for our village

I never pass that area without remembering those days
it brings a wave of yearning over me
for it was a time of togetherness and delight
a wonderful era of perfection
in a circle woven from allegiance
and I can still taste the everlasting promise of youth

It's a Barnum and Bailey world—just as phony as it can be
But it wouldn't be make-believe if you believed in me

CLASSMATES

Linda, Judy, Jack and Mick
Donna, Joe and Peg
Charlie, Gary, Mar and Mark
but not a soul named Gregg

flirts and brainiac's
jocks and nerds
never the twain shall meet
comedians, heart-throbs, lovers and haters
all made our class complete

basketball stars and football pros
baseball heroes too
gave cheerleaders cause to jump for joy
and reasons to pursue

those naughty boys whose purpose was
to conquer virgin queens
those catholic girls who start too late
went way past sweet sixteen

we're doctors, lawyers, nurses too
perhaps some music shakers
I think that one of those Theta guys
married a NY film-maker

so here's to the class of 67
the best of the best for sure

we've still got Solvay in our blood
for that there is no cure

let's join in a toast to all that remain
and to our talents much magnified
someday we'll all be together again
when we meet on the other side

It was only high school after all, definitely one of the most bizarre periods in a person's life. How anyone can come through that time well-adjusted on any level is an absolute miracle!

HELL NIGHT

some wrote on us with permanent markers
while others broke raw eggs on our heads
blindfolds offered more uncertainty
as we made our way through the hellish
path to membership
buckets full of spaghetti pretended to be worms
and we were ordered to run our hands through the
illusion
squeezing bananas while our imaginations ran amuck
the higher-ups barked orders and we followed like sheep
for we were finally able to see a light at the end of the tunnel
we happily bit the onions
and chewed the Alka-Seltzer
we recited the Greek alphabet
and accepted the paddling as part of the deal
some cried and some laughed
while some ran away in fear
but I remember that feeling at the end
that incredible feeling of belonging
it was an honor—to be part of that special sisterhood
devoted friends who shared a commitment
and the promise of kinship
and we met and prayed together
and shared our darkest secrets
we laughed and cried
and promised to be family forever
Alpha Omega
the beginning and the end
bringing us that much-needed protection

from the cruelty of high school
some of us are no longer here
but we all remain devoted representatives
there is no more jealousy or vindictiveness
no more competition or ill-wishing
all that remains is the comradery
from that age of innocence
and the heartfelt love for our sisters

Sorority life is a loyalty—it's rushing and campaigns, meetings and songs
It's traditions and formals—and a lifelong pledge.

WOODS ROAD

it was one of those streets that reached
immortality
for me, it held some of the best
and the worst
memories of my life
lifelong friends lived there
and I would walk to their homes
always finding safety and comfort
I fell in love for the first time
on that street
and in typical school girl fashion
carry that memory still
ever so enraptured within me
we played piano
and went for walks
and because those friends lived so close together
we would all meet
on one of the porches
sitting for hours never realizing we were making memories

and like a satanic curse
love took one of ours
and we sat horrified watching from afar
as they took her from us——forever
leaving us with such mixed emotions
for the one who remained also held a piece of our hearts

mostly I have happy memories
of that iconic street

field days and parades
first love and lasting friendships
proms and semi-formals
and the music—-the beautiful innocent music

it was a place of invulnerability for me
and its memories remain embedded in my soul
like a blaze of sunset that will forever bring peace to my heart

Encountering the mystery of first love is life altering
And it won't be the last—but it will last forever

SANDY POND (and memories of Joe Fournier)

this quaint little beach town was full of
deep dark secrets
seniors flocked there carrying coolers full of beer
and any other inebriant we could steal from our homes
girls in bikinis and guys in baggy swim trunks
we buried ourselves in the sand
and picnicked on bologna sandwiches and wise potato chips
after a few hours
we loved the one we were with and
though so many lies were spoken
very few were remembered
promises flew like broken boomerangs
never to surface
and we bid farewell to the sins of the day
when we left the Pond behind

I walked with Joe on the beach near the marina
we were drunk and laughing at each other
his jet-black hair was glistening in the sun
and I can still see his green and black shirt
my head was on his shoulder when I told him I felt sick
and he stayed with me
until the vomiting stopped
he never judged
he probably knew me better than anyone
and he still thought I was all that
he picked me up the next day and we spent some time together
and I remember looking into his green eyes and thinking

he was probably going to be president one day— *God, he was brilliant*
and I loved him but not like he wanted me to
Lord, what I wouldn't give to re-write that piece of my history
we teased each other about our antics together
and I missed him when he left for Berkley
was I so wrapped up in myself that I never saw his sadness
never heard his unspoken cries for help
maybe there was something in the water at Sandy Pond
for it claimed a few more seniors throughout the years
I can't go back there—not without him
but I will—someday—when we finally meet again

****Perhaps earth was the wrong place for him. I think it always was*

DONNA PIENKOWSKI'S GRAND-MOTHER

she was an angel
she was legally blind—
but she was an angel
we would skip school and meet at Donna's
one by one we would call the school
pretending to be a parent
and making up illnesses
that could have killed a warrior
I think I had malaria once
poor Linda had scarlett fever
and we would hide from her Grandmother
and she never suspected

we drank Kool-aide
and ate whatever Donna had in the fridge
walked to Tanzy's for ice cream
and if Linda had the car later on
we'd cruise the streets
honking the horn
and just being goofy

sometimes Donna's house was so full
of teenage girls
the noise alone should have given us away
but it was as if we were meant to be there
meant to make those memories
and we were bonded together
like partners in crime

at times I think Donna's Grandmother
knew the truth all along
perhaps she recalled her youth
and those friends of yesteryear
and though her eyes couldn't see anymore
her heart remembered
and she let us enjoy life
as she once did

If you know your Grandmother, you know unconditional love

RAH RAH SISS BOOM BAH

nothing can fill me with nostalgia faster
than the memories of cheerleading
navy blue pleated skirt
white wool sweater with a big block letter **S**
wool sweat socks and canvas sneakers
and jocks——gotta love the jocks
the sound of athletic shoes squeaking on the gym floor
and that ever so distinct smell of sweat that permeated the air
megaphones and orange and blue pom-poms
stag jumps and splits
it was like being famous for a few hours every week

I was the perhaps—the biggest cheerleader for my teammates
I would watch in awe when our Captain would perform a jump
she literally looked like *Baryshnikov* on steroids
and some of the girls practically flew as they arched their backs
and reached for the sky
me—on the other hand—got a few feet off the floor and tried to
look tall
which for those of you who knew me then know that was no
small feat

I was so proud to wear that uniform
to be a part of that special group of girls that could turn a few heads
to lead the crowds with the chants and cheers that we believed
actually helped
win the games
and I remember singing our Alma Mater
not really digesting what those words meant

but I understand now, and I cherish those times

and when those games were over—win or lose
I was filled with a sense of self-esteem
and pride for not only for my squad
but for the athletes that we represented

it was the best of times
for what could possibly be better than being a cheerleader
and being 17
it was the one time I had the world by the ass—and I didn't even
know it

> *Cheerleading was my thing—but then so was
smoking and drinking*
> What can I say??? I'm flexible like that

PEP RALLY

we gathered around the bonfire
inhaling its scent like a drug
for what could be better than a crisp
autumn night set aside for this auspicious occasion
and we cheered and applauded
singing the praises of the football team
the night was full of pledges
and anticipation
as we cheerleaders promised the crowd
a winning season
and couples held hands
and took advantage of the special ambiance
that perfect blaze offered
there was a feeling of togetherness
and for just for that one night
the cliques disappeared
there were no dividing lines
no popularity contests
for we all had only one thing on our minds
school spirit

I stared across the crowd in an attempt to catch
his roving eye
but his glaze was focused on another *(as usual)*
and I remember walking home with Joe
we talked and laughed
he told me my cheerleading sweater smelled like
the bonfire
and he told me I was an idiot to waste my time

on that other guy
and now when I look back on that night
I can still remember the aroma of burning
wood
and the feel of warmth I got
not from the fire
but from the incredible friendship he offered me
it was one of the most special evenings of my life
and I wonder if I'll ever feel that way again

My spirit belonged to the orange and blue——and you

YOU CAN'T GO BACK AGAIN

Or—what I'd do differently

I'd study harder
and worry less about being one of the popular girls
I'd go to med school and become a surgeon
and definitely choose my relationships more carefully
perhaps I wouldn't love so intensely or give up so easily
and I'd try to be a better friend
I'd go to church more often
and read my dad's bible
I'd never smoke
and it's for sure I'd flaunt my intellect instead of hiding it
I'd become a blonde at a much earlier age
for it's given me the confidence I so sorely lacked
I'd spend more time with my parents
I'd listen more attentively to my friends and family
and I'd try my best to be a kinder, more loving person
I'd wear a different gown to the Senior Ball
one that showed off the person I am
it would be pink and green and made by *Chanel*
full of whimsy and irony and a total show stopper
and my shoes would be by *Jimmy Choo*
in shades of pastels with stiletto heels
and I would have danced every. single. dance.
and realized even back then how very short life can be
I'd be kinder to those classmates who were invisible
inviting them to join us for lunch or whatever
and I'd be less judgmental
because we were all special—we were all so very talented

and I would be more accepting of those who collected stamps or those who built model cars
I'd admire others clothing
even if it didn't come from *Flah's or Addis or Wells and Coverly*
I'd read more *Shakespeare*
and instead of reading *The Catcher in the Rye* 10 times—I'd read it 20
and I would savor each and every moment of my 17th year
as if it were the best year of my entire life
because it will never again be as memorable
as when you're in it——wishing it could last forever

   ***How strange that a 17-year-old would think the world is against them*
    when in fact it is the only time made especially for them

I GOT THE MUSIC IN ME

it was 1967 and I had a lot to say
Van Morrison's *Brown Eyed Girl*
was totally me back in the day
Sinatra's *Somethin' Stupid*
could practically be my bio
and Pickett's *Funky Broadway*
was the place I wanted to go
that *Sweet Soul Music*
always put me in the mood
cause *All you need is love*
explained this senior's attitude
Frankie Valli's sentiment screamed
Can't Take my Eyes off you
and *Gimme Little Sign*
could thrill me through and through
I used to think *It Must be Him*
that could fill my heart with joy
but when ole *Jimmy Mack* hit home
Baby Love boy oh boy!
Love is Here and Now You're Gone
was the story of that year
but it was *Kind of a Drag*
to *Light my Fire*
and then simply disappear
that day I turned *A Whiter Shade of Pale*
and headed down *Penny Lane*
was the day we became *Happy Together*
and I'll *Never My Love* complain
I often wondered *How Can I Be Sure*

and should I go *Up Up and Away*
but then I found *Incense and Peppermint*
and the *White Rabbit* led the way
I'm a Believer said it all
when I was seventeen
and there was *A kind of a Hush*
all over the world
when our music made the scene

***Remember, this was an era where you were defined by*
the music you listened to and the clothes you wore—
gotta love the 60's

SMOKER'S ROAD

it was a sort of prestigious zone
for those of us that indulged in the evils of nicotine
and we flocked there after lunch
smoking as many cigarettes as possible
in the allotted amount of time
never giving a thought to the adverse effects
or the horrific smell
for it was a sign of the times
everyone did it
they did it in the movies
and on Broadway and at funeral homes
at movie theaters and it was just *so cool*
and I remember that line up looked like the who's who of Solvay High
regardless of the weather we trekked there
cheerleaders hiding the ever-pure uniform
with navy blue rubber raincoats
and trying our best not to soil the white sneakers
sometimes that line would be 35 people long
with enough smoke to infect the strongest of lungs
yet we gave no thought to disease
for we were far too young to worry about our health
it was a celebrated road
one of societal acceptance
camel smokers and other non-filtered tough guys
shared the spot with those girly-girls puffing away
on Ultra-thin 100's or Virginia Slims
and you didn't worry if you were out of cigs
it was perfectly acceptable to share a smoke with a friend
not a problem at all

and we met on that dirt road daily
inhaling not only the pollution of the cigarette
but the unwavering friendship of that fellowship
and like every other bad habit
some of us walked away from that pathway
smoke-free and unscathed
and some of us still crave the essence of that trail
for its attraction was as addicting as the nicotine

****Some people smoke to put nicotine in their veins*
and others smoke to put a cloud between them and others

THE EXTRORDINARY, ILLUSTRIOUS ONONDAGA LAKE

on Sundays when the hot weather hit
we'd visit Onondaga Lake
our entire extended family would picnic there
but it wasn't an ordinary picnic
we went to Willow Bay armed with pots and pans
coolers filled with Molson Beer and Pepsi
pitchers of homemade lemonade and iced tea
and kettles full of sauce and meatballs
the children ran around free and unsupervised
as adults prepared the enormous spread
and for us it was just another Sunday dinner
except it was outside
grandparents sat in chairs high atop a hill
looking down on us and occasionally barking out orders in Italian
they were served first, of course and while we ate, they critiqued
the food
after the meal the adults washed the dishes (no paper plates for us)
and we prepared the table for dessert
while other picnickers indulged on assorted melons and fruits
we feasted on Italian cookies and pastries
but Onondaga Lake held other enchantments
it was the place to be during the falsely acclaimed submarine races
teen lovers would drive there just as the sun set
sometimes stopping at Heid's for a hot dog or a Cooney before
the carnal activities began
more often than not you could find those couples in steamy make-
out sessions
trying their best not to get too carried away

and it was euphoric
at least stories that followed were
there were always two versions: his and hers
one was full of romance and promises
and the other full of sexual fantasies and false pretense
yet for some of us———it was lifechanging

when visitors speak of that *Lake*
they speak of disappointment because of its pollution
questioning why all that natural shoreline was never repaired
but for those of us that were "regulars" there
it was a beautiful, picturesque lagoon
that existed exclusively for our pleasure

****I was always a black swan floating in the
middle of that forbidden lake*

SMILE AND SAY CHEESE

Daniel Sauro wasn't just a photographer
he was *thee photographer* back then
anyone who was anybody wanted to be photographed by *Sauro*
weddings, showers, engagements and senior pics
he was the man to see
his work was state renowned and though he was pricey
he was, after all—the best of the best

his studio was located downtown
and once you entered you were immediately surrounded
by breathtaking photographs of brides, babies and lovers
all captured in the most perfect poses
in vivid, resplendent color for all the potential customers to see

we sat apprehensively in our black off the shoulder drapes
waiting to become part of the infamous
for a brief moment in time, we were almost star-like
as we posed for the master in hopes of becoming forever immortal
at least on canvas

and he tilted our heads—this way and that
telling us just where and how to look so that his expertise could shine
because it was as much his talent that needed to be recognized
as our beauty
it was—as the world would eventually see it—-a masterpiece to
be exalted
we were merely pawns in his universe

and we did as we were told so he could bring out our allurement

all of us duped into believing we were the epitome of beauty
and we passed around his "wallet size" finished products
exclusively signed by the guru
and pretended we were remarkable
for just a moment in time

    ***There are no bad photographs—that's just how your face looks sometimes Abe Lincoln*

BEARCAT ECHOES

back in the 60's
if you never made it into the *Post Standard*
this high school newspaper was the next best thing
there were gossip and advice columns
athletic schedules
academic achievements
and—of course—all the school news that was fit to print
not only did we female reporters have to be sharp intellectually
we had to look sharp, too
we sported white "sailor hats" that boasted our titles for all the school to
see
"echoettes" became a catch-phrase
while the sailor hat became more prestigious with every passing year
when each new edition was ready, we would roam the halls
attempting to sell the latest low-down
of course, it was cinch if you knew your name or picture was in there
otherwise—25 cents was better spent elsewhere
yet we were all so proud to be a part of that assemblage
proud to represent our school
and though none of us were what you'd refer to as "crackerjack
reporters"
we put out a hell of a gazette
though most newspapers are a bad habit
(the reading equivalent of junk food)
the *Bearcat Echo* had quite a following
we believed we were making great contributions to society
we complicated the simple and simplified the complicated
we injected humor where there was none
and we popularized the unpopular

I wish I had known then that I could have motivated people
that writing was a true talent and I was blessed
that everyone reads but few understand
and that journalism can provide a ring-side seat to those who seek
knowledge
perhaps I would have attempted to reach more people
but I am eternally grateful for the opportunity given to me
let's face it—none of us threatened *Walter Kronkite* with our
talent
but we had a hell of a good time pretending to be notorious

        ***Never trust a newspaper or a mirror*

LET US ENTERTAIN YOU

it was a time of remembrance
and a time of celebration
The Foreign Student Show was a much-publicized theatrical
jackpot
right smack in our little village
we sang and danced
laughed and grew closer together
and this gathering of talent became a tradition that will forever live
on in our hearts
I have only to close my eyes to become a part of the chorus line
again
and every time I hear the song *Volare* I am immediately filled with
elation
we offered entertainment that was intended to be ingested like
fine food
and a little applause was all we needed to push us to an encore
it was exhilarating
for we discovered hidden talents in our classmates that we never
knew existed
but the most incredible discovery of all
was the way we all came together to make the show a success
we showcased ourselves in the form of musical geniuses
artists, comedians, thespians and mimics
we tugged on the heart strings of our audience with songsters so
talented
it was as if an angelic choir made a home on our stage
and we reveled in the ovations and the praise
for it awakened the headliner in all of us

after the show we celebrated
and we spoke of its success for months to come
reminiscing and replaying those special moments
and in that time, we pretended to be someone else
we took on the part of the person we wanted to be
if only for a brief moment in time
for who we are usually depends on who's looking at us
or at least who we think is looking at us
because we are all just playing a role
just masquerading as that perfect character
on a stage we call life

****All the world's a stage and the men and women merely players William Shakespeare*

Che CAFETERIA

ah—lunch time in the cafeteria
what could be more delectable
than a crisp lettuce sandwich
or spaghetti cooked to the consistency of porridge
and if you really wanted to treat yourself
how about a day-old bologna sandwich on the ever popular
Wonder Bread
some of us had better ideas even back then
never a lover of peanut butter
I joined the lunch crowd with luscious leftovers
consisting of sausage peppers and onions
the fragrance alone was enough to bring the strongest football player
down to his knees
and what could be better than thick slices of Italian bread
dripping with olive oil and loaded with salami, provolone and
roasted reds
sometimes I was lucky enough to have a mouthwatering home-
made pastry
baked with love by my incredible Mom
yet for a mere 27 cents there were those who chose
a steamed hot dog, limp green beans and applesauce
wow! a meal fit for a pauper

yet our lack of sophistication — at least in our palates
never kept us from enjoying that special time
regardless of what we ingested
it was never about the food
we sat and talked and shared our meals
dipping our plastic utensils in and out of our classmate's dishes

for the sustenance didn't come from the nourishment
it came from those we shared our entrées with
we feasted on the comradery and the kindness of our cohorts
and it more than satiated us
and we grew from the branches of togetherness
that remain intertwined even today

****If only some foods were illegal, I
would love them even more*

THE EVER-DREADED DETENTION

suffice it to say
the absolute coolest kids were in detention
being a frequent visitor
I can attest to this personally
my ever-popular eye rolling and constant chatting in class
landed me in that after school prison more than a few times
and instead of using the time constructively
I would doodle away the hour
scribbling some mindless dribble
usually practicing writing my name combined with the beau of the
month
I got to know some of the *Tucci's* in that room
most of whom were on lock-up for smoking in the boys' room
or some other unforgiveable evil-doing
like wearing black leather jackets, pegged pants and *Tucci* boots
those rebels were the ones that we pretended to write off
yet I'm sure I wasn't the only one who shared a fantasy or two
about those east-side hoodlums with the slicked back hair
they rode motorcycles even back then
and wore t-shirts tucked into skin tight jeans
an all too obvious pack of camels found a home in the sleeve of
their shirt
rolled tightly into perfection for all the world to see
some of them even displayed a tattoo (unheard of then)
and the preppy guys made fun of them
while the virgin girls flirted with them
and never the twain shall meet?
only it did meet—
and the results were usually a bit less than pure

that room held the nonconformists, renegades and malcontents
and some of the most intelligent, independent thinkers I have ever met
one of the regulars was a poetry lover and he would write small verses for me
on ripped pieces of lined note paper——*(I had a secret crush on him)*
and the lessons I learned in that room
were less about school and more about life
and I don't regret a single moment of those punishments—
it was — for me— a glance into another dimension of living

****Detention is just a part of high school——with weapons!*

THE NY STATE FAIR

because the fair was headquartered in our village
we teenagers had a front row seat to the festivities
we would walk down bridge street past Carmen's
to the entry gate
and once inside, an entire new world was there at our feet
I found little joy in the buildings
nature was never a turn on for me—still isn't
so visiting pigs and cows and chickens was the absolute *last* thing
I wanted to do
yet my love for the midway was immeasurable
the rides, the games, the food
and oh—those ill reputable carny people
I stared at them almost in disbelief—for they were an assortment
of people like I had never seen
gold capped teeth, tattoos, bandannas on their heads
each of them chanting aloud and tempting us to try their crooked games
the gigantic stuffed teddy bears were every young girl's dream
and if she were lucky enough to have a boyfriend who could win
one for her—
well—she pretty much had it all
darts and basketball enticed the boys—3 tries for 50 cents
while the girls begged for time in the tunnel of love
and we walked—around and around
smoking and checking out the faces in the crowd
smiling at strangers and sampling every single bit of "fair food"
we could possibly get our hands on
pizza fritte from *the Villa,* funnel cakes, sausage and peppers
London broil and huge cylinders of cotton candy
some of us would flash a fake ID and indulge in a few beers

and others found contentment sipping a Pepsi or chocolate milk

and when night fell we drifted into pairs
holding hands and maybe arms around each other's waists
I can still remember the aroma of fried food in the air
and the mellow sound of *The Young Rascals* in concert
no responsibilities—not a worry in the world
and the sheer exquisiteness of a cheeseburger and fries
it was the absolute perfect atmosphere for teenage abandonment

****We were a bit too middle class to fit in with the carny people So we just hung with them while they were in town*

FLIRTING AS AN ART FORM

it was one of my favorite things to do
I had flirting down to a science
maybe start with a casual compliment
hey—love your shirt
add a little tease—not too much
bet that shirt is really comfortable
follow that with a seductive smile
and just a playful touch—nothing aggressive
listen to him as if he were the president
omg—that's soooo interesting
be seductive—but innocently so
and always leave him wanting more
you absolutely must be confident in yourself
and draw a little attention to your lips
you know—lip gloss works wonders
and if you're really brave—just tell him you're interested
now, while I took flirting to another level
I didn't exactly hold the record for most dates with a 17-year-old girl
I spent a lot of nights crying in my pillow—alone
but I attribute that to the fact that with the exception of an incred-
ible few—
I had horrid taste in boyfriends
for some inexplicable reason I repeatedly chose boys who
weren't interested in me
perhaps it was the challenge that intrigued me
or the fact that I was more content without them but loved the chase
add the that the fact that I had (have) the attention span of a
toddler before nap time
and that pretty much sums it up

for all those boys back in high school that played along with me
I'd like to thank you
for giving this small-town pudgy girl some much-needed confidence
for telling me I was "cute" or "pretty" because it brought my
tenacity to a new level
you taught me poise and fearlessness when I needed it most
and whether or not it was real: your interest gave me faith in
myself and what I had to offer
you taught me not to settle and that self-worth was everything
and you gave me the courage to fall in love
so for those of you that think flirting is not an art: think again
it takes a determined little girl to face rejection—to face humiliation
and come out on top
and for that—I am eternally grateful to every boy that pretended I
made a difference

****I have many roads to travel—but I
prefer the one that leads to you*

THE MIRROR HAS TWO FACES

looking in the mirror I saw a pudgy, little short girl
with pale white skin and deep-set brown eyes looking back
my hair was a mousy brown and cut pretty short
I was, without a doubt—the epitome of uncomplicated
this simple, naïve young girl appeared somewhat short-sighted and
gullible
but those who took the time to know me
found a marvelous sense of humor and a devotion to friendship
that was unsurpassed
I wore the best clothing yet it would have made a better home on
a taller, thinner girl
and though I secretly prayed to be a leggy blonde—it was never
in the cards
and so at 17 I continued to look 15 and each morning as I faced
that cruel mirror
the plain, round faced adolescent peered back
as any teenage girl would do, I primped and pampered myself daily
a bit of blush—-tease the hair
love's baby fresh and a smear of lip-gloss helped a bit
at least until bumping into a sophisticated young woman who was
5'8" tall
shoot me in the foot
I absolutely hated that mirror and it wasn't until many years later
that we became friends
I did grow a couple inches and came into my own, but—
thank the good lord for makeup, bleach, high heels and stores like
Casual Corner and Flah's
so when I run into an old school mate who tells me I haven't
changed a bit

trust me—that's not a compliment
because change I most certainly did
perhaps the mirror can't reflect the wisdom that made me more attractive
that piece of glass can't project the joy of a first love or the agony of a first heartbreak
nor can it showcase the scars that have healed from the inside out
or the hundreds of disappointments and mis-fortunes I have encountered
at 17, that imager tells nothing of inner beauty or personality
it reveals only outward symmetry and at that age—it's barely visible
those years we spent making friends with the mirror pass quickly
and before you know it—we are enemies again
for now it displays the years of wear and tear and stress
and we—once again—wish for that 17-year-old to reappear
that youthful glamour girl who was too busy wishing for tomorrow to recognize her own beauty
and so we challenge the mirror and sometimes we win
but for those times that the cruel, harsh truth is too much for us to handle
remember to search for your inner beauty—and make that piece of glass your friend

       ***Mirrors constantly show you what you lack— not what you really have*

SURVIVAL OF THE FITTEST

I sometimes wonder how we survived the 60's
we lost hundreds of coins in gold shag carpet
had no bottled water or helmets or knee pads
and we played outside the entire day no matter how hot or how cold
we knew nothing of cable tv and we only had about 5 channels
and we had rotary phones that you actually had to dial
and we did it without helpers like *Alexa or Siri*
our parents had avocado green or harvest gold appliances
they collected *S&H Green Stamps* and we helped lick em and
stick em
we helped our Mom's when they hosted a *Tupperware* party
and if we did a good job we might get rewarded with candy
cigarettes
we never worried about getting fat in the summer
because we had no air conditioning and we literally sweated off 5
pounds a night
most places were closed on Sunday—it was, after all—a day of
rest—-*no church—no nothin*
we rarely had soda—it wasn't allowed and fast food was a treat
saved for special occasions
we played with metal Slinkies, easy bake ovens and Barbie and Ken
we had hula-hoops and glass ball clackers and banana seat
bicycles *(ouch)*
some of us joined fan clubs—we were devoted to the Monkees
and the Beatles
there were no video games so we played kick ball or dodge ball in
the street
you haven't lived until you've been hit in the face with that red ball
and it was usually thrown by a 250 pound "boy" who claimed it

was his way of flirting

there were no credit cards—*omg!!* and homemade treats were allowed in schools

we watched cartoons for hours on Saturday morning on wooden console tv sets

and if we wanted a hot snack—we had to use the stove cause there was no microwave

you dreaded first aide because you got Mercurochrome or Camphophenique

and if you complained of an upset stomach you got Brioschi *(yuk)*

everything had a closing time, virtually nothing stayed open 24 hours

and there were no drive-thru windows anywhere

girls had mood rings that sometimes cracked in the cold—not dangerous at all

and boys put baseball cards in the spokes of their bike wheels for noise effect

we walked—everywhere—-and we never locked our doors

if we stayed up late at night, we saw the local tv stations sign off at midnight

and it played the National Anthem—every. single. night.

parents could send their kids for cigarettes with a note

and if you didn't have the cash—you could open a "charge-account" at the corner store

I was traumatized by the *Huckster* (just thought I'd throw that out there)

and my heart breaks for those "youngsters" that never experienced what we did

it was the coolest time ever!

***Outdoors—the original PlayStation*

ST. CECILIAS

I always loved the silence in the church before mass began
it was an opportunity to reflect and communicate silently with God
a peacefulness fell upon the congregation
and it was one of the few times I actually felt "holy"
the beauty of this house of prayer was breathtaking
and the aroma that filled the air transported those that attended mass
to another dimension of belief
sometimes we frequented mass in groups
and though we spent little time actually praying
those were my favorite times
we took up an entire pew
all of us girls pretending to be spiritual and righteous
when in reality we were searching the congregation for boys

after communion we would sneak out
sometimes walking together or sitting in one of the cars
and we talked about everything
        and we spoke of nothing important
yet it was what we loved to do

church when you are 17 is a parental subpoena
for most of us it was just a Sunday morning ritual
and as I look back at those innocent days
I remember that feeling of peacefulness
that feeling of being sheltered from everything evil
and the comfort in knowing at least one thing in our cockeyed
teenage life was invariable
how I would love to congregate one more time with that group of girls
perhaps finding a bit more significance in the mass and its offerings

and just for an hour or so
give thanks for surviving this journey
because without *his* divine intervention
I seriously doubt any of us would have made it this far

****In heaven, all the interesting people are missing!*
Friedrich Nietzsche

A WANNA BE

we all have dreams when we're seventeen
and though some are crushed by those envious rivals
most of us strive for excellence in spite of the "nay-sayers"
the girl that you thought was ugly and beneath you
now saves lives as an Oncologist
and the boy that was voted class nerd
by those who refused to let him in their fraternity
is now a member of a more prestigious club known as *NASA*
and has spent at least one of his vacations on a different planet
that beauty queen you so wanted to look like
has been married 3 times
and drinks herself into a stupor night after night after night
for her loneliness consumes her as she still reaches for yesterday
still wanting to be the prom queen—still wishing she could get by
on her looks
now picture that jock all the girls had a crush on
who every day in high school was considered a hero and a hunk
well—he's got bad knees now and can hardly walk
and that black wavy hair—he's lost it all

seventeen is surreal
seventeen can cut like a knife and break hearts
yet for some of us seventeen was perfection
it was a time of hope and promise
and those lucky few who fulfilled their dreams
can still remember that mythical age and smile
for they strove—even then—to make a better future

and as for me—my talents eluded me for so many years
and my intellect blossomed later than most
but I am finally comfortable in my own skin
and when I dream of seventeen, I dream of a fantasy time
a time of popularity and friendship and discovery
and if I were to be seventeen again—just for a moment
I would grab the world and hold on as tightly as possible
because the next time around—I'll force that axel to spin in a
different direction
and reach for the stars a hell of a lot earlier

****Don't cry because it's over—smile because it happened*
                                          Dr. Seuss

THE MUCH-LOATHED GYM SUIT

to say it was ugly is an understatement
picture a one-piece navy blue short "romper"
much like a flour sack with elastic around the ballooned legs
you could put this thing on Jennifer Lopez—
and it would make her look ugly—and that's pretty hard to do
though we were forced to wear it twice a week
it didn't seem to bother us since we all looked dreadful in it
because in the gymnasium—none of us were beauty queens
Ahhh—gym class
I still have nightmares about that friggin rope—
"come on LaValle—shimmy up that rope"
seriously? the only time in my life I could shimmy
is if I were on the dance floor—and then it was questionable
let's see 10 push ups
now I realize that there were girls that could accomplish this
but the only thing I could ever "push up" was a popsicle
you want me to run how far?
bitch, please!
I'm only running if I'm being chased—and then it depends on
who's chasing me
perhaps that revolting suit was supposed to transform we girls into
athletes
it never worked on me
I think I had to purchase a new one on a monthly basis
because I kept "losing" mine
and God forbid one of the boys saw us in that monstrosity
that would be a fate worse than death
some of us would have done anything to get out of gym class
and wearing that suit

I know for a fact that one of us had her period for 365 days non-stop
and my sprained ankle lasted 2 years
unfortunately, there was always a spare suit
so saying you forgot yours was a dead end
at any rate—
the memories of my athletic prowess—or lack of
are pretty much tainted by that gym suit
yet I still smile when I think of those times
when all we cared about was being together
and we never gave a thought about how weird we looked
because we were too busy being seventeen

****You're hanging from a rope, you're dressed hideously and
girls are throwing dodge balls at you and snapping towels—
and you're just trying to survive those 40 minutes*

SOLVAY POOL

bare feet on wet cement
led to a "basket room"
where for the price of a mere 25 cents
you were allowed admittance to the locker room and pool
a small band with a key found a home on your wrist
and you stashed your clothing in a locker that had probably been
used by thousands
and never, ever cleaned
a quick shower and it was off to that perfect public lagoon
for a day of fun in the sun

God—those lifeguards were cool
they sat perched in their special chairs way up high
looking down on us as if we were another species
and as we splashed around with total abandonment
I'm sure a few of us were thinking of pretending to drown
just to get a few minutes of attention from one of the guards

we would spend the day at that oasis
splitting our time between swimming and laying on the hard
cement
just a thin beach towel for relief from that blistering concrete
yet the lack of comfort never seemed to bother us
for it was a time of enjoyment and togetherness

that pool was our home for the summer
we would walk there and back in the scorching summer heat
with nothing but a towel, a quarter and maybe a bagged lunch
and we were filled with pleasure and contentment

our tanned youthful bodies sparkling like little berries in the hot sun
submerged like fish in that chlorinated water

our fingers and toes wrinkled and over-hydrated
only proved to accentuate the beauty of our youth
and we frolicked as if we were children of privilege
with exemption from all that was insignificant or trite
and most of the misfortunes of those teen years
were washed away in the magic found in the elixir of that pool

****The water doesn't care how old you are*

TAKE FIVE

he taught me to play the *Brubeck* song on his piano
along with other jazz favorites
and I became one of his followers
his world was one of music and entertainment
and while he introduced me to that special world
he also became a best friend and confidante
and though I was filled with admiration and respect for him
it was his best friend I fell in love with

I loved being at his home
for his family became a part of me
and the hours spent there were deliriously happy
sometimes we would sit on the porch
just watching the cars go up and down the street
and while the house next door belonged to my first love
I was equally happy at either place
and though each home offered a different kind of love
both houses became almost an addiction

sometimes I remember those innocent days
bittersweet as they were
and I can still feel the happiness
and that strong sense of belonging and acceptance
and a feeling of nostalgia washes over me
bathing me once again in sentiment and infatuation

and just for a brief moment in time
I wish I were back there
playing that piano

or in the arms of my first love
for I would capture that time for all eternity
putting it in a special place I could visit whenever I felt insecure or
small
for a first love of anything is meant to be savored
and remembered with a passion that can never die

****first love is the sweetest and also the most bitter. Sweet
because we'll always remember it—bitter because there will
never be another like it*

MY SUMMER AS A PARKS AND RECREATION SPECIALIST

back in the summer of 66
I became an expert at boondoggle and watching children in the
"baby pool"
for $1.25 an hour, the village where I lived
employed me as a park and recreation specialist
now as cool as that title is and as hard as it is to believe
it was not one of my favorite positions
picture it: *Solvay Pool 1966*
about 25 babies and toddlers screaming at the top of their lungs
parents with cigarettes hanging from their mouth screaming back
at them
a large round cement pool with about a foot of water and a
fountain in the middle
kids running like banshees and me trying to control them
bloody knees and elbows and lots of Band-Aids—sometimes
found floating in the water
and every once in a while, one of the older kids
would attempt to jump over the fountain
leaving me to administer first aide to body parts I was totally
unfamiliar with

in an attempt to calm things down
we would have two hours of crafts for the older children
which basically consisted of creating boondoggle key chains
and painting rocks
honestly—at times I wished I could have woven a boondoggle
muzzle (or two)
the children were somewhat more subdued

and for a couple hours I had a reprieve from bloody limb treatments

following the craft portion of my day
(and me wishing I were 18 so I could drink)
I would instruct the 4 and 5-year-old kids on pool safety
they responded to this educational period
by kicking, screaming, biting, vomiting and pulling each other's hair
so much for pool safety—I was more concerned for my own safety

now if you're asking yourself why I remained at such an outra-
geous position
the answer is simple: *they gave me a whistle*
that whistle represented authority and I blew it frequently and
with conviction
not one child responded to it but nonetheless, it was cool as hell
I finished the day with a sense of accomplishment
pleased as all hell that no children were destroyed on my watch
and me (and my whistle) survived another day

****If someone whistles at me, I don't turn around*
I'm a Lady——not a dog

POMP AND CIRCUMSTANCE

a time of celebration
a time of reflection
a time to plan and dream
and a time of pride and accomplishment
and today, I rise to applaud us
full of pride and bittersweet memories
as we make a way to our future
a future I hope will be worthy of us
a future that will lead us to that special path
hopefully the one less traveled
for we are deserving of the very best
and I wish for us love and success
wisdom and empathy
understanding and the importance of family

remember:
life is not a dress rehearsal
we can be anything we put our minds to
we will play hard, work harder
and face the world unafraid while savoring every moment of this
new adventure
and as we move that tassel to the other side
we reminisce of days gone by
of stately halls and SAT's
bon fires and gatherings
we cling to those friendships that will be ever remembered
and our hearts break a little as we bid farewell to the past four years
goodbye to sororities and fraternities

and to those teachers who paved our way

we are the future
and though at seventeen we still tremble with uncertainty
perhaps not ready to sacrifice our innocence
we accept the challenges and prepare to enter a new world
for we are the world's "shinning stars"
and it is our time to finally shine

****Accept no one's definition of your life——define yourself!*
Robert Frost

GUESS WHO'S COMING TO DINNER?

it was a simpler time in 1967
things were uncomplicated and transparent for a while
yet it was a time of germ warfare and flower power
and it was a time of racial confrontation
but in our small village we knew little of this prejudice
we were far more interested in the capture of the "Boston
Strangler"
Viet Nam was at the top of the news
and while we watched Ed Sullivan
blacks and whites alike were fighting for our freedom in that
dreadful war
where as many as 15 U.S. helicopters were shot down
in. one. single. day.
color meant nothing to those risking their life
and it meant nothing to those of us with empathy or compassion
in my humble Italian home
dinner was shared with any and all the friends we invited
my parents entertained them regardless of race
and there was no judgement passed
for all they needed to know was that we enjoyed their company
and that if we cared enough about them to invite them into our home
they must be "good people"
it was a time of peasant food and family gatherings
and while we discussed trivialities such as the marriage of Elvis
and Priscilla
Richard Speck was executed for the murders of 8 student nurses
there were race riots in Florida and Illinois and New York
and the Supreme Court disallowed interracial marriages
Paul McCartney admitted taking LSD

and Sidney Poitier was idolized in "To Sir with Love"
and as I fantasized about being Barbra Streisand in "Funny Girl"
the conflicts and the race riots continued
whites and people of color were killed by the thousands
we listened to the Beatles sing "All you need is Love"
and we celebrated the nomination of Thurgood Marshall as the
first black justice
and as we broke bread with those we loved
malevolence continued to grow
and that simple, uncomplicated time soon became nothing more
than a memory
and our hatred and bigotry spread like a cancer
turning even the most exquisite colors
into a pigmentation of horror

*****Whisper words of wisdom——let it be*
The Beatles

THE INNOCENCE OF SEVENTEEN (for JF)

he drove a green Pontiac
and one of the doors stuck
but like a true gentleman
he opened it from the inside and helped me in
we saw *The Graduate* and I could feel myself blushing
he seemed cool as a cucumber
afterword he took me for ice cream
and we ate it in his car
savoring each and every bite
but all I could think of was the inevitable kiss good night

he walked me to my front door
and we were still talking and laughing
and when he finally kissed me I felt a kind of relief from the
tension of the evening
it was a tender and sweet kiss
and I can still remember him telling me I was beautiful
now when I recall that evening
it seems I remember even the way he smelled
and his green eyes almost penetrating my soul

when I saw him at school on Monday
I smiled at him
and he winked because he knew though we may not be in love
we were kindred spirits and we would be forever connected

I dream of him habitually
sometimes waking in a cloudy hazy of sadness
for his death was so unbearable

so painful
I can hardly accept it still

and for those that knew him
and understood his level of intellect
his feel for humanity and his compassion for those less fortunate
you are truly blessed
for I believe with all my heart
that he was never meant to walk among ordinary people
like you and me

****Love is the sweetest and slowest form of suicide*

SHE'S A DANCING MACHINE

Miss Augustine did it all
tap, ballet and modern jazz—she ruled the dance world
always with a scarf around her neck she commanded respect
and the woman had the patience of a saint
shuffle ball change—tap tap tap
smile everybody
there wasn't a girl in our village who wasn't familiar with her
at the beginning of each class, she would collect our money
for a mere pittance each of us enjoyed the fantasy of becoming a
Prima Ballerina
or the world's next *Ginger Rogers or Cyd Charise*
and for a half hour twice a week we danced with total abandonment
twirling and whirling and tapping to our hearts content
black patent leather tap shoes shining brightly clicking and clack-
ing loudly
with black grosgrain ribbon tied in a perfect little bow
little pink ballet slippers hugged our leotard clad legs
while we tippy toed and pointed our toes all over the studio
some of us were meant to be there
for dancing was in our blood
and some of us were forced by our mothers——
in hopes of achieving the epitome of gracefulness
but little girls become young ladies
and dancing for Miss Augustine in your teens was a whole other world
she was a perfectionist
gone was the patient saint-like teacher
replaced by a wand pointing command shouting prima donna
not only did the price go up
but so did her expectations

not so much fun anymore
and so the age old dream of becoming a *Rockette* vanished with
puberty
out was the spindly body of a child
and in came boobs and thighs
tap shoes were traded for sneakers
and that ever-popular studio became just a memory
as we discovered that boys were much more fun to dance with
but whenever I see Fred dance with Ginger
I remember her and her scarf
and what I wouldn't give to do one more *time step*
with the master

*****Remember, Ginger did everything Fred did—only better!
Cause she had to do it backwards—and in heels!*

THE BEST DRESSED STUDENTS

poor boy sweaters and penny loafers
were pretty much the rage
dress code warned of girls wearing pants
never happened in that day and age

converse sneaks and white sweat socks
with a pleated navy skirt
mohair sweaters and button-down blouse
a standard uniform for the flirt

guys with pegged pants and cardigans
and an occasional smooth bow tie
were sure to turn a young girl's head
or at least earn a wink from her eye

goby boots or tucci boots
or a leather jacket with some chains
separated the good from the real bad boys
and those who were merely mundane

Wells and Coverly, Casual Corner
Flah's and Addis too
outfitted more than a few of us
and they were just a preview

Wassong's gowns and Lerner Shops
Park Brannock for our shoes
gave most of us a confident boost
to us kids from Syracuse

madras shirts and monogrammed blazers
suede jackets trimmed with leather
we sure turned some heads way back when
man—we had it ALL together!

*****I love a man who knows how to dress—
And I love him more when he pays to dress me!*

SHELTER FROM THE STORM

around the corner from the old high school
was a wooded area with a worn path that if followed would lead
to the pool
this somewhat hidden area was a well-known spot for all kinds of
gatherings
the high school guys would meet there frequently
maybe to smoke or throw back a few brews
the shelter—as it was known—was usually off limits to us girls
sometimes we would cut through to save a few steps
and every once in a while, one of the guys might take a girl there
for a quick make out session
but normally it was reserved for "the boys"
card playing and swearing were the normal at that man cave
as well as playing "chicken"
a ridiculous game consisting of placing a lit cigarette between the
forearms of two guys
and the first one who flinched—-well, he was the chicken
needless to say, a lot of high school guys sported scars on their arms
there were all kinds of hiding places there, too
for nature has a way of creating special nooks and crannies
perfect for camouflaging packs of smokes and cans of beers
but mostly *the shelter* was a gathering place for a group of boys
who were—at the time—inseparable

this somewhat picturesque area was also home to a lot of family picnics
we would trek there by the dozens—parents and children—
cousins, aunts and uncles
setting up tables and paper tablecloths, folding chairs and coolers
with tons of food and drinks

celebrating our heritage and closeness
never paying any mind to our primitive surroundings
and it was a shelter like no other
for it brought so many of us together
perhaps in different ways yet the bond was there
that little tree-laden spot is a part of our history
and who among us doesn't smile when the memory returns
of that little piece of nature that sheltered us from all that was
threatening

> ***The earth has music for those who listen*
> *William Shakespeare***

SEMI-FORMALS, PROMS AND OTHER SHINDIGS

first it was weeks of torture wondering if someone would ask you
and—would it be the one you wanted to ask you
after that awkward moment it was on to dress shopping
overpriced "frocks" in every color imaginable hung from racks in stores
tempting and teasing with promises of fairytale endings
and price tags that put parents into temporary shock
and let's not forget the accessories:
shoes, purses, jewelry and makeup
not to mention getting the hair done—in an up-do, of course
this in itself was a major event
after washing the hair, it was set in rollers the size of large beer cans
you then sat for 45 minutes under a scalding hot (loud) hair dryer
this part was usually entwined with a verbal barrage of obscenities
that you thought no one else could hear because you were literally on fire
then came the teasing of the hair after which enough hair spray
was applied
to require a gas mask
the hair was then smoothed into a bee-hive and sprayed again—
only until it wouldn't move in a strong tundra—-aaah——the
price we pay for beauty
(and so much for your date running his fingers through your
hair—fat chance)
your date arrives at your home, and is immediately blinded by the
flash of your Dad's camera
after 74 snapshots were taken, your Mom drags out your baby
pictures
by this time your deodorant is melting and you're embarrassed
beyond belief

your feet are killing you, your hair resembles *Marge Simpson's*
and your panty hose are cutting off your circulation
to top it all off, your strapless bra is somewhere around your knees
making your beautiful, ultra-expensive gown look like a maternity
frock
at this point, any attempt to move would probably be fatal
cause either the hair's fallin down, the shoes are comin off, or the
bra is history
after 20 trips to the bathroom and a compromise of sorts with
your gown and your bra
you attempt to dance with him
he smells like *"Grey Flannel"* and he tells you how beautiful you
look
and suddenly—-nothing else matters but being in his arms

I don't remember the anguish or the embarrassment or the foot pain
what I do remember is for a few short hours I was a princess
and in spite of the blisters on my feet and the rat's nest on my head
it was one of the best nights of my entire life

****You can get married two or three times, but Prom night—*
That's a once in a lifetime experience

UGLY DUCKLINGS

dreams are dreamed by beauty queens
whose followings aren't what they seem
and those ugly ducklings who filled the pond
swam beneath those who went beyond
and caught the eyes of senior boys
and small-town socialites who laughed at us
had nothing at all to even discuss
and who did we eventually blame
for Valentines that never came
or teams that never called our names
while jocks and beauties claimed their fame

at seventeen

and for those of us who knew the pain
while waiting for dragons to be slain
and with nowhere else to run
we melted into nothingness and came undone
and those gorgeous girls with perfect smiles
were envied by those with inferior styles
inventing boyfriends out of need
while at home we'd crumble and bleed
wishes to be a part of the crowd
who floated high above the clouds
and those who wore old hand-me downs
were frowned upon like circus clowns
and when our names were never called
which of us were not appalled

by clicks of popularity
and those that lacked sincerity

at seventeen

and those of us with acned faces
who lacked in higher social graces
came into our own but in a torturous sort
when that frivolous age did finally abort———
at seventeen

> ***For dreams were all they gave for free to ugly duck-
> ling girls like me*
> *Janis Ion*

OBSESSIONS @ SEVENTEEN

quarterbacks, the Beatles and Charlie Brown
Twin Trees, Lou's Diner and Bianchi's
Marble Farm's Ice Cream
    Carvel's pineapple milkshakes
        and pizza—any pizza; *love pizza*
shopping for shoes, baby pink lipstick
bowling and cheerleading
jocks, musicians and Friday nights
poor house west
    Fairmount Fair
        and smoking Parliament 100's
sleepovers, swimming, long walks and W.O.L.F.
ford mustangs, Lake George and Hewitts
sorority, girlfriends, green-eyed boys and pep rallies
stuffed animals, siblings, neighbors and the state fair
French fries, Carrol's, convertibles and puppies
crushes, fraternity pins, loafers, Jean Nate' and Canoe
date parties, semi-formals, senior balls and proms
homemade lunches, mashed potatoes and chocolate chip cookies
Sassoon haircuts, ice skating and kissing
    cheeseburgers on Italian bread
      pickles
        and Tanzella's
Pepsi, Kool-aide and popsicles
holding hands, visiting colleges and writing letters
driving, beaches and sandy pond
Vicky's, 45's, the Rolling Stones and Petula Clark
Casual Corner, Well's and Coverly and Flah's
mohair sweaters, raspberry berets, Tom Jones and The Monkees

graduation, foreign student show, assemblies and Shakespeare
(ok—this one may be just me)
Edgar Allen Poe, Snoopy and Kalett Theater
Steve McQueen, Valley of the Dolls and Sidney Poitier
looney tunes, Bonanza and Marlon Brando
meeting him, falling in love and parents
never looking back
    never looking forward
        never ending hope

****And when I met you, I was instantly obsessed. There was no sleeping or eating or existing without you. That's what an obsession is. You really have no choice in the matter!*

WISHING ON A STAR

we all have goals at seventeen
maybe medicine was your desire
or engineering or accounting
some of us wanted to be housewives
while others dreamed of fame and fortune
lawyers and actors
secretaries and mechanics
or maybe an artist's life was your fantasy
and as we entered our world of uncertainty
few of us continued down the path of choice
for there were twists and turns along the way
marriage and babies
        disappointments and divorce
sickness and unexpected road blocks
and we cried as we remembered our dreams
and we wished that we could start over
but the world kept on moving
and the axel turned with lightning speed
and those wishes we made on far away stars
disappeared in clouds of regret and remorse

yet at seventeen the fantasies are real
we know little of disappointment and disillusion
and though the path we walked was sometimes paved with
heartache
we persevered   we endured
        we survived
and as we watch our children and grandchildren
choose the path they believe is perfect and full of promise

we remember the road we traveled and the wishes we made
and we silently pray that their journey is easier than the one we
took
and that the stars they wish on hang just a bit closer to earth
a bit closer to reality
    a little easier to grab

and though we secretly want to join their journey
to try that path again
    turn back the clock
we smile and offer encouragement
and ready ourselves for yet another bumpy ride

    ****We would be sorry if all our wishes were granted*

NOT A CARE IN THE WORLD

it's such an incredible feeling——
no responsibilities
no rent to worry about or bills to pay
someone to cook for you and make sure you're safe
warm loving arms to comfort and protect you
buy clothes for you and make a home for you
teenagers have it all

and yet we dream of moving out
starting our own life and being an independent soul
our own place
        our very own home
                adulting

and when we were seventeen
did we appreciate all we were blessed with
or were we so wrapped up in our childish egos
that we took for granted the very things that kept us alive
the love that will forever be unsurpassed
and the devotion bestowed upon us by our parents

and today with positions reversed
what we wouldn't give for another hug from Dad
another opportunity to laugh with Mom
or just a few more words of wisdom from those ever-insightful
Grandparents
who shared their wisdom as we sat—ever so content—-listening
to their past adventures

not a care in the world did we have back then
and we slept in sheer contentment
all the time thinking of nothing but ourselves
and praying time would pass quickly
so that we could leave the abundance of our youth behind
and enter the world of obligations, culpability and anxiety

ah—what fools these mortals be
for what did we ever know at seventeen?
and why oh why—did we ever want to bid farewell to our youth?

> ***"Youth ends when egotism does; maturity
> begins when one lives for others."*
> *Hermann Hesse*

CONFESSIONS OF A VERY SHORT GIRL

I longed to be a dancer
with legs as long as stilts
but when you're only 5'1"
it's not the way you're built

try finding pants that fit just right
and don't need a 3-foot hem
they're sure as hell not made for me
but who am I to condemn?

those designers who think that all the girls
should have bodies like Tyra Banks
but what about us little ones
who don't fit in those ranks

we dream of walking the runway
and wearing gorgeous clothes
but we can't even buy a pair
of normal pantyhose

so much for Chanel or Gucci
Valentino or Jimmy Choo
their clothes are made for leggy gals
that we have to look up to

try reaching for that proverbial star
or top shelf for a pan or a pot
good luck not driving too close to the wheel
or sinking a perfect jump shot

so out the window went my dream
of modeling or dancing on stage
I guess I'll have to be content
to never look my age

so while you chics with legs for miles
show off the gams like Grable
I'll show my talents elsewhere girls—
by cooking you under the table!

        ***Sure, Ginger Rogers could dance—but did
                 she ever make sauce for Fred?

THOSE PHENOMENAL THETA OMEGA GUYS

it really was the fraternity to end all fraternities
and they were some of Solvay's finest
Theta Omega was a not only a collection of guys with different
personalities
but different backgrounds and looks as well
and each and every one of those *"Theta Guys"* were all that and
a bag of chips
they had a certain *je ne sais quoi* that followed them everywhere
tall and lean
        short and stocky
they were all blessed with the gift of gab and personality plus
and they all had a way with the gals
and if you were fortunate enough to be invited to one of their date
parties
well—weren't you just the luckiest of the lucky
baby blue button-down collar shirts
        dreamy cardigans
                and oh, those sexy pegged-pants
and what about those much-envied fraternity pins?
there wasn't a Solvay girl alive that didn't dream of wearing one
on her collar
now, as a former *Theta Omega* pin wearer (or maybe a collector)
I can definitely vouch that "being pinned" was one of the greatest
feelings ever

I remember, fondly, so many of their smiling faces
Mickey and Joe
        Jack and Richie

Chris and Mike
and I remember ever so vividly
their humor and their kindness
for in spite of the reputation that usually preceded them
every single one of them had a heart of gold
or at least that's the way I prefer to remember
those flirty, manly, loveable, playful, AWESOME
Theta Omega guys

****So—you want to be a chic magnet??? Be a "frat boy"*

MEMORIES OF DARROW AVE

my childhood was quintessential
and the street I grew up on was sheer perfection
we played kick ball in the street
learned to balance on skate boards
rode bikes and homemade scooters
and spent time at each other's homes
blessed with the world's best neighbors
I ended each day with a smile on my face
and hopes for another day like the one before

and when we entered our teens
we did it together
for we were all so close in age
that we shared much more than friendship
we were a family
and we had a special bond
we shared snacks and lemonade
candy from Balduzzi's
and some of the world's best baked goods
created especially by *"Grace and Anne"*
we all ran to my Dad when he came home from work
and he would catch every one of us and throw us in the air
and we laughed and laughed
and then we stayed together till dark (or until Ernie whistled)
and did it all again the next day

it was a piece of history that us "Darrow Ave kids" still carry with
us
similar to a *Norman Rockwell painting*

that iconic street had it all
including the magnolia tree to end all magnolia trees
to this day its beauty and aroma remain unsurpassed
and it lived smack dab in the middle of my front lawn
there will never be another time in my life when I felt so loved
for every day I was surrounded by comrades and partners
best friends and playmates
and I celebrated life with the best of the best
and still carry a piece of each and every one of them
deep in my heart

****If I had a flower for every time I thought of you—I
could walk through my garden forever
Alfred Tennyson*

GOOD BYE TO INNOCENCE

so quick to leave our innocence behind
those days of purity and virtue
how we hurried to chase the storm
and face those stumbling blocks
yet then—we were oh so reluctant to look back
for we threw caution to the wind
and gladly faced the unknown
and there were demons and dragons
villains and fiends
and some of us needed rescuing or freedom from exploitation
and we left that cradle of safety
left the shelter of family
and with great expectations we flew
our first solo flight
into that sometimes-frightening world of adulthood
and we were faced with grownup matters of contention
no more the free child
        no more running for refuge to loving parents
there was no turning back
and we longed for those simple years
those years that brought happiness and uncomplicated wishes
and who—-we wondered—would protect us now
from those monsters that used to live under the bed
those beasts that we thought only lived in fairy tales
and the days grew shorter
and the darkness came quicker
and our prayers turned to more conventional needs
as we apprehensively embraced an entirely new personification
and we reached for those days of youth

and we remembered the ease of it all
the laughter and the friendships
and those sublime dreams we thought would come true

goodbye sweet seventeen
farewell to those days of splendor
visit my dreams now and again
oh, how I long to go back and be an innocent again
for just a moment in time

****All things truly wicked start from innocence*
Ernest Hemmingway

EPILOGUE

Writing this book was especially enjoyable for me. It filled me with nostalgia and gave my sometimes "less than astute memory" a much-needed jolt. And——it was just plain fun!

High school is a special time in everyone's life, but I think that our Senior year may be the most memorable. It is a time to prepare for what's next in life and a time to absolutely grab on to the last bit of school and all its offerings.

When I remember Solvay High School, it is with the highest regard. I am instantly filled with happiness when I remember those stately halls and the people that strolled them each and every day. How I loved to change classes, for it gave me a quick opportunity to see friends and favorite teachers and to create a bit of mischief along the way. Was there anything better than an impromptu assembly or an early dismissal? How about Christmas vacation or long weekends?

The promises we made back then have lived forever in our hearts. Though we said goodbye to so many companions, we remained friends with even more. We bonded into adulthood and even watched our extended families grow. It seems almost impossible that so much time has passed, but here we are watching our Grandchildren travel the same paths—still full of twists and turns and oh, so many dead ends!

I wish we had buried a time capsule back in the sixties. Can you imagine getting together and opening that chest?? I know just what we'd find, for it would be full of memories and love and some of the most incredible trinkets————*Mohair sweaters and Goby boots, Varsity letters,*

Fraternity and Sorority pins, Keds, Locker combinations and gym suits, Yearbooks and Bearcat echoes, Pia Patrone and Mike Campolita (hahaha)

I find myself sharing school stories with my children and grandchildren more frequently—perhaps because I enjoy the memories so very much. I want them to know what a wonderful time it was, and that for me it was a time that I will forever cherish.

> *I think of the 60's and I think of us*
> Of what we used to be
> And now that we have come full circle
> I close my eyes and see
> That seventeen was the year that was
> The year we said farewell
> To childhood hopes and silly dreams
> And places we used to dwell
> Goodbye old friends I'll miss you so
> But drift apart we must
> Keep in touch and think of me
> And in our friendship trust
> That time can never separate us
> Or the bonds that we have formed
> For Solvay roots run deep they say
> And can weather any storm

Marianne

www.ingramcontent.com/pod-product-compliance
Lightning Source LLC
Chambersburg PA
CBHW072027150726
47999CB00002B/771